STYLE
AND
INTERPRETATION

*An Anthology
of 16th-20th Century Keyboard Music*

Edited with Introductions and Notes by

HOWARD FERGUSON

Volume 1: Early Keyboard Music (I)
England and France

OXFORD UNIVERSITY PRESS

MUSIC DEPARTMENT

LONDON · NEW YORK : TORONTO

STYLE AND INTERPRETATION

FOREWORD

STUDENTS OF THE PIANO are often so pre-occupied with the acquisition of technical skill that they do not give enough thought to stylistic, textual and interpretative considerations. This is a great mistake, for technique is only a stepping-stone and remains meaningless until it is allied to musical understanding. Innate musicality is the first requisite; but this must be cultivated, not only through contact with a wide variety of music, but through a knowledge of the way in which style and interpretation changes from century to century and country to country. Such facts are quite as important as technical skill, and if a student ignores them, his playing, however brilliant superficially, will never penetrate to the core of the music.

In this anthology Dr. Ferguson has made an outstanding contribution to the clarification of these problems. His absorbing survey, written from the twin viewpoints of a composer and performer, is imaginative and lucid, and covers an extensive period in a way which has not, I believe, been attempted before. Everyone who is interested in keyboard music and its performance should find these volumes endlessly stimulating and instructive.

February 1963

MYRA HESS

Printed in Great Britain by Halstan & Co. Ltd., Amersham, Bucks

Volume 1.   Early Keyboard Music (I): England and France

CONTENTS

KEYBOARD MUSIC *(continued)*

GRADED INDEX

PREFACE

MUSICAL NOTATION is of necessity imprecise. It leaves much to the innate musicality of the performer, and much to his knowledge of the various conventions and usages of different periods. These last are often blandly ignored by performers—particularly those brought up in a mainly Romantic tradition—with the result that we hear Bach fugues played as though they were Brahms intermezzi, early rhythmic conventions ignored, and ornaments interpreted without any realization that they may mean entirely different things to different composers of even the same period.

The present anthology aims to point out a few of the more important of these problems of style and interpretation. It cannot in the nature of things be comprehensive, for the subject is as vast as the art of music itself; but if it helps to make some players aware that such problems exist and are worth trying to solve, much of its purpose will have been achieved. At the same time, Volumes 1 to 4 form a miniature history of music written for keyboard instruments (excluding the organ) from the mid-16th to the 19th century. The first two volumes together cover the two centuries from c. 1550 onwards, Volume 1 being devoted to composers from England and France, and Volume 2 to those from Germany and Italy. Since they deal with the same period, and with music written mainly for the virginals, the harpsichord or the clavichord, their Introductions are interdependent and should be read in conjunction with one another. Volumes 3 and 4 are both self-contained, and are devoted to, respectively, Classical piano music from Haydn to Schubert, and Romantic piano music from John Field to Brahms. Within the volumes, or sections of a volume, composers are arranged chronologically; and graded indexes are provided for the student who may wish to approach the pieces in order of technical difficulty.

The musical texts are printed as nearly as possible as the composers left them, the source of each being given on its title page. Where an autograph no longer exists, or is for some reason unavailable, either a contemporary manuscript copy or the earliest reliable printed edition has been used. No editorial phrasings, dynamics, pedallings or fingerings have been added. All these aspects of performance are, however, discussed in broad outline in the Introductions, and are often referred to in the Notes that appear before each individual piece. Editorial accidentals, rests, and notes are printed small, editorial slurs and ties are indicated thus: ‿ and other editorial additions are printed in square brackets.

With regard to phrasing, dynamics and pedalling: it is essential that the student should be able to see what a composer really did write, so far as this is possible, if he is ever going to learn how to interpret the existing marks correctly and supply the missing ones in an idiomatic and stylish way. It is also advisable that he should form an early habit of working out his own fingering; for though certain broad principles may be laid down, only the player himself can tell which of several possibilities is the best as far as he is concerned. From every point of view, therefore, it seems preferable to start with an unadulterated text. The student can then cultivate his musical imagination by learning to interpret it for himself.

A partial exception has been made concerning ornamentation. To avoid endless page-turning and reference to tables, a suggested realization of each ornament has been added above or below the stave at its first appearance in every piece.

The music in the various volumes was written for a variety of instruments—the virginals, harpsichord, lute-harpsichord, clavichord, fortepiano and modern piano. Anyone who has access to several of these will be lucky indeed; but even if the student is restricted to the piano alone he should not grieve unduly, for the important thing is that he should play and enjoy the works and others like them. In learning to do so in an idiomatic way he will be opening new fields of exploration and delight for himself, and at the same time enlarging and deepening his understanding of the music he already knows.

ACKNOWLEDGEMENTS

More than half the pieces in this volume have been taken from first editions, or in one case a manuscript, owned by the British Museum. For the use of these, and for permission to publish, I should like to offer my warmest thanks to the Trustees. My thanks are also due to the Director of the Huntington Library, San Marino, California, for permission to use the three pieces which I have taken from the facsimile of the Library's unique copy of the first edition of *Parthenia*. Permission has also been kindly given by the Syndics of the Fitzwilliam Museum, Cambridge, for the use of two pieces from the *Fitzwilliam Virginal Book;* by the Council of the Royal College of Music for the use of the pieces by Blow and Arne; and lastly by the Bibliothèque Nationale, Paris, for the use of Dandrieu's *La Lyre d'Orphée.*

Several of my friends have given generously of their time to reading parts of my MS, and have made valuable suggestions for which I am extremely grateful. In particular I should like to thank Professor Thurston Dart (who has also kindly given permission for the use of the quotation on p. 7), Dr Frank Mannheimer and Mr Yfrah Neaman.

Howard Ferguson
LONDON, 1961-62

INTRODUCTION

The Instruments

A GENUINELY IDIOMATIC style of writing for keyboard instruments other than the organ first appeared in the middle of the 16th century in England, where it was developed to an astonishing degree during the flowering of the Elizabethan and Jacobean virginalists. Thereafter the initiative passed elsewhere: at first to France, with its great school of harpsichord composers headed by Chambonnières; then to Austria and to Germany, where a vigorous early tradition was crowned by the unmatched masterpieces of Johann Sebastian Bach. Italy was less concerned with keyboard music; yet Domenico Scarlatti, living in Spain and Portugal and relying more on his own idiosyncratic genius than on the example of his predecessors, evolved a style of keyboard writing unique in its originality and brilliance.

These four great schools of keyboard writing provide the material for the first two volumes of this anthology. Before discussing the music itself, however, it will be helpful to consider for a moment the instruments for which it was written, so that we may grasp their basic characteristics and mechanism, and understand in what respects they differ from the modern piano. The ideal way to gain this insight is to play on either old instruments or modern reproductions of them; for one learns more about, say, a Scarlatti Sonata from an hour's practice on a harpsichord than from reading any number of books. But unfortunately it is not always possible to do this; so it often becomes necessary to fall back on written descriptions of the instruments and their characteristics. These can never be more than a second best; but at least they are more helpful than the easy assumption that all early instruments were no more than squalid makeshifts, and quite unworthy of the unfortunate composers who had to use them.

If the organ is excluded, the earliest keyboard instruments can be divided into two families: (a) the Clavichord; and (b) the Harpsichord group, which includes the virginals, spinet and some others less important.

The Clavichord

(French: *clavichorde;* German: *Klavichord;* Italian: *clavicordo, manicordo*)

The clavichord is in many ways the most perfect of all keyboard instruments. It is oblong in shape, with the keyboard set in one of the long sides and the strings running from left to right of the player. The action is extremely simple. At the far end of each key is a small brass blade, or tangent. When the key is depressed the tangent rises and strikes the string, at the same time stopping it like the finger of a violinist's left hand. The section of string to the right of the tangent vibrates to produce the note required, while the section to the left is damped by a piece of felt wound round the end of the string. When the key is released the tangent falls back, the whole length of the string is damped by the felt, and the note ceases to sound. There is no sustaining pedal.

Though so simple, this action can produce wonderfully subtle results; for the clavichordist, unlike the player of any other keyboard instrument, remains in direct and continuous control of the string as long as the key is depressed. This makes possible the finest tonal and dynamic gradations; and a slight up-and-down movement of the finger will even produce a very expressive vibrato (German: *Bebung*).

Against this unique sensitiveness must be set the clavichord's lack of power. Its tone is so delicate that it would scarcely be heard in most concert halls; and in ensemble music it cannot stand up to other instruments. Thus it is essentially a solo instrument for use in small rooms. In such surroundings its remarkable expressiveness is soon as apparent as its unexpected ability to suggest a wide range of dynamics.

The earliest surviving clavichord was made in Italy in 1543. But an earlier instrument is described in a mid-15th century manuscript compiled by Henri Arnaut of Zwolle, physician to the Duke of Burgundy; and still earlier models undoubtedly existed several centuries before that. Though its popularity began to wane in England, France and the Netherlands towards the end of the 16th century, it remained in use until the early 19th century in Italy, Spain and Germany, largely as a practice instrument for organists.

The Harpsichord (*including the Virginals and Spinet*)

(French: *clavecin (épinette);* German: *Klavicimbel, Clavicembalo (Spinett);* Italian: *clavicembalo, gravicembalo (spinetta)*)

The essential difference between the clavichord and the several instruments included in the harpsichord family is that the strings of all the latter are plucked by quill or leather plectra instead of being struck by brass tangents. Furthermore, the basic mechanism of even the simplest harpsichord is much more complicated than that of the clavichord.

On the far end of each key of a harpsichord rests a slim upright piece of wood called a 'jack', the top of which is level with the strings. (Sometimes there is more than one jack, as will be seen later.) Projecting from the side of the jack, and normally resting below the strings, is a plectrum of quill or leather. When the key is depressed the jack and plectrum rise, the latter plucks the string in passing, and the whole string-length vibrates to produce the note required. When the key is released the jack falls back to its original position (an ingenious device allowing the plectrum to pass the string silently), the string is damped by a small piece of felt attached to the upper part of the jack, and the note ceases to sound. Again, there is no sustaining pedal.

Such a plucking action gives a much louder and more brilliant sound than that produced by the tangent of a clavichord. It is also much less sensitive to variations in the player's touch, and cannot match the clavichord's wide tonal and dynamic variety or its characteristic vibrato. A second manual was probably originally added to the harpsichord to simplify transposition; but it was soon adapted to the more important purpose of extending the tonal resources of the instrument. Further sets of strings were added, together with the jacks and plectra needed to operate them; and hand-stops (later these were operated by pedals) enabled the player to use whichever set of strings, or combinations of sets, that he required.

This tendency towards expansion can be seen in the specification of a surviving English harpsichord of 1755, which possesses

2 keyboards of five octaves each;

3 sets of strings: one of 8-foot pitch and one of 4-foot pitch (that is, sounding an octave higher than written) actuated from the lower keyboard; and a second, contrasting set of strings of 8-foot pitch worked from both keyboards. This contrasting 8-foot register is provided with a second set of jacks, placed closer to the ends of the strings, which are worked from the top keyboard only and produce a sound like a lute.

4 hand-stops: one each for the 8-foot and 4-foot registers of the lower keyboard; one for the contrasting 8-foot register operated by both keyboards; and one for the lute effect on the top keyboard.

With such a specification many different permutations of registration are possible, so that the player can obtain a considerable variety of dynamics and tone-colour. But unlike the clavichordist, he cannot make a long and gradual crescendo or diminuendo. His changes of colour and dynamic, apart from small ones due to variations in touch, must always be made in sudden steps. Furthermore, if these involve a change of hand-stops, and not merely a shift from one manual to the other, they will always take an appreciable time to effect. Modern instruments have, of course, pedals instead of stops, and can thus make changes of registration without this break. There is no indication, however, that any of the great composers for the harpsichord ever used such a device or relied on it for their music.

The instrument described above is a true harpsichord, shaped like a narrow grand piano, with strings stretching away from the player. The other two important members of the harpsichord family, the virginals and spinet, are different in shape and have only the simplest type of harpsichord action. The virginals (sometimes called virginal, or a 'pair of virginals': cf. a pair of scissors) are oblong like the clavichord, while the spinet is a roughly wing-shaped polygon. The strings of both run from left to right instead of away from the player; and as each has only a single set of strings and jacks, no changes of registration are possible. It must be remembered, however, that until the late 17th century the word 'virginals' was used in England to describe all the instruments of the harpsichord family and perhaps even the clavichord too. Thus the famous collection *Parthenia or the Maydenhead of the first musicke that euer was printed for the Virginalls*,

c. 1612/13, was not intended exclusively for the true virginals, but also for any of the other instruments.

The earliest surviving harpsichord was made in Italy in 1521. But the mid-15th century manuscript of Henri Arnaut of Zwolle, already mentioned, describes an earlier type of instrument; and another appears in an illumination of the Duc de Berry's *Très belles heures* of c. 1416. The harpsichord's heyday was from the 16th to the 18th century, and it remained popular throughout Europe until it was finally superseded about 1780 by the more expressive and equally powerful fortepiano.

Tonal characteristics of the older instruments

If we compare the tonal characteristics of the older instruments with those of the piano the following facts stand out:

1. The clavichord is unique in its subtlety and delicacy. Like the piano, it can produce a continuously graded range of dynamics: that is, a crescendo, a diminuendo, and different dynamics simultaneously in different voices. It is extremely sensitive to variations in touch, and can even, unlike any other keyboard instrument, produce a vibrato. Its power, however, is strictly limited.

2. The harpsichord, on the other hand, is comparatively powerful. It has a brilliant, incisive tone, the strength and colour of which may be altered either by a change of manual or by means of stops (latterly pedals). These alterations can only be made in clearly defined steps; and any involving a change of stop must have required, on the instrument of the classical harpsichord composers, an appreciable time to accomplish. Unlike the clavichord and the piano, the harpsichord cannot produce a continuously graded range of dynamics, or a long crescendo or diminuendo. It is limited to a single dynamic level at a time, except for the contrast that can be obtained by playing on different manuals with each hand.

3. The tonal characteristics of the spinet and the true virginals are somewhat similar to those of the harpsichord; but neither instrument has any stops, so the player has only a single tone colour at his disposal. (N.B.: in 16th century England the name 'virginals' included *all* the instruments of the harpsichord family and possibly also the clavichord.)

4. None of the older instruments has a sustaining pedal.

Playing early music on the Piano

Now that we have some slight knowledge of the characteristics of older instruments, we must pass on to consider the interpretation of the music that was written for them. And since comparatively few people are lucky enough to be able to play on harpsichords and clavichords, we should also consider how the music may best be interpreted on the piano.

Happily it is no longer thought necessary to 'arrange' or 'transcribe' early music before it can be used by a pianist. Our present-day approach is well summed up by Thurston Dart, who writes:

Each instrument must be true to itself, and it must not try to ape the others. The harpsichordist must not fuss with the stops in order to try to make his instrument imitate the gradual increase and decrease of tone possible on the piano. The clavichordist must play delicately and expressively; a clavichord must never sound like a dwarf harpsichord. The pianist must resist the temptation to use octaves in imitation of the harpsichord's 16′ and 4′ stops, for the effect on his instrument can never be the same . . . The performances must also be stylish; they must be illuminated by the fullest possible knowledge of the special points of phrasing, ornamentation and tempo that were associated with the music when it was first heard. The performer has every right to decide for himself that some of these special points are best forgotten; but he must at least be aware that they once existed, and that they were at some time considered to be an essential feature of a pleasing performance. (*The Interpretation of Music*, p. 166-7.)

When we set out to follow these admirable precepts we immediately come up against a major problem: for one of the first things we notice when we open a piece of music of the 16th, 17th, or even early 18th century, is that it contains virtually none of the indications of tempo, phrasing, articulation and dynamics to which we are accustomed. The explanation is simple. The accepted conventions regarding these matters were so well known by the performers of the day, when composers themselves were always intimately concerned in music-making, that there was no need to waste time and ink by writing them into the copy. If a doubt about any point should arise, the composer himself, or someone who knew him, would be at hand to provide the answer.

As we are less fortunately placed, we must try to work out the relevant basic principles for ourselves, with the help of whatever contemporary evidence we can find.

Tempo

The first problem that confronts the student of early music is to determine its tempo. This has troubled others before him, for we read in the introduction to Purcell's *A Choice Collection of Lessons*, 1696, that there is 'nothing more difficult in musick then playing of true time'. As a step towards solving the problem it will be helpful to consider for a moment some aspects of musical notation that are now obsolete.

During the 16th and 17th centuries notation was passing through one of its periodical phases of transition. It was moving towards the present-day system, in which the relative value of notes remains constant (1 breve=2 semibreves=4 minims, etc.), a time-signature shows how many notes of a given denomination occur in a bar, and a tempo mark indicates the speed at which they should be played. At the same time it was moving away from the old barless proportional system, in which the relative values of notes did not remain fixed, but were indicated by means of various symbols, the forerunners of our time-signatures.

In the proportional system the various note-ratios were shown *c.* 1600 by the following four symbols:

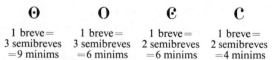

| 1 breve= 3 semibreves =9 minims | 1 breve= 3 semibreves =6 minims | 1 breve= 2 semibreves =6 minims | 1 breve= 2 semibreves =4 minims |

The symbols denoted not only the metrical structure of a piece but also its approximate tempo, for the speed of a movement was settled by reference to the semibreve as a standard time-unit. Modifications of these standard speeds were accomplished by the use of further signs,

e.g.:   ◑   halved the note-values of **O**

    ¢ or Ɔ   „   „   „   „   „   **C**

    ◑   „   „   „   „   „   ¢

$\frac{2}{1}$ (*dupla*, diminution) meant o = previous ♩

$\frac{1}{2}$ (*dupla*, augmentation) meant ♩ = previous o

$\frac{3}{1}$ or 31 (*tripla*, diminution) meant o o o = previous o

$\frac{3}{2}$ or 3 ($\begin{pmatrix} sesquialtera, \\ diminution \end{pmatrix}$) meant   o o o = previous o o

(It will be noticed that the symbols **C** and ¢ have survived in modern notation. The numerals, on the other hand, are unrelated to their apparent modern equivalents; for the modern time-signature $\frac{3}{2}$ means three-minims-to-a-bar, not three-in-the-place-of-two; and $\frac{2}{1}$ now means two-semibreves-to-a-bar, not minim-equals-previous-semibreve.)

The virginalists' use of the signs was extraordinarily muddled, and different sources often give different signs for the same piece of music. Those most frequently encountered are: **C** and ¢ for simple and compound duple time; $\overset{\text{◑}}{3}$, ¢ and $\overset{\text{¢}}{3}$ for simple triple time; and 3 for brisk triple time. 31 or 3 in conjunction with a symbol was commonly used for a moderate triple time such as a *Galliard*, while 3 standing alone indicated a quicker triple time such as a *Coranto* or *Jig*.

Another element of notation then in a state of transition was the unit of musical movement. It is a curious fact that the duration of notes tends to lengthen over the centuries—the breve, as its name implies, was originally short instead of very long. Hence we find that the normal unit of movement shifts every now and again to the next lower note-value. At the time of the virginalists it was hovering between the minim and its present-day value of a crotchet. This can be seen even within a single collection of pieces such as *Parthenia*, c. 1612/13, where four of the five Pavans require a beat of c. 80 to the crotchet, whereas the fifth (No. 10, Bull's *Pavana: St Thomas Wake*) requires the same beat to a minim.

It is most important to remember this ambiguity, for it often makes music look to our eyes much slower than it should in fact be played: e.g. Bull's *Gigge*, vol. 1, p. 26, and Frescobaldi's *Gagliarda*, vol. 2, p. 48.

As to the actual time-value of the unit: Mersenne in 1636, Christopher Simpson in 1665, and several later writers equated it with the human pulse, which means roughly 80 (*cf.* the Pavans mentioned above). But it would be a mistake to expect all music to fit unfailingly into such a pre-ordained straight-jacket, however convenient it might be to the theorist; so we must in practice allow the unit to vary somewhat.

By the end of the 17th century time-signatures had taken the place of mensural signs; and at first they too had connotations of tempo. Purcell's *A Choice Collection of Lessons*, already mentioned, gives an explanation of their significance which may be tabulated thus:

COMMON TIME

C = 4 crotchets in a bar: a very slow movement

₵ = 4 crotchets in a bar: a little faster

◐† = 4 crotchets in a bar: a brisk and airy time

TRIPLE TIME

$\frac{3}{2}$ = 3 minims in a bar: played very slow

31 = 3 crotchets in a bar: played slow

3 = 3 crotchets in a bar: played faster

$\frac{6}{4}$ = 6 crotchets in a bar: for brisk tunes like jigs and passpieds

These signs do not always provide as much help in determining tempi as we might wish, for composers used them almost as inconsistently as the mensural signs. In Purcell's Suites, printed in the very same volume, we find $\frac{3}{2}$ ('a very slow movement') used for a brisk *Hornpipe;* and ₵ applied to an *Alman* marked 'very slow', which clearly requires the sign **C**. (A confusion between **C** and ₵ is very common, and the two signs will even be found in different instrumental parts of the same ensemble piece; so the student must always be on the look-out for it.)

When we leave English music we find that the problems of tempo begin to clarify slightly. The French harpsichord composers often prefixed their pieces with words such as *Tenderly, Gaily, Quickly* or *Slowly*, sometimes implying a speed through a mood, and sometimes stating the speed directly. At times, however, these directions are merely intended as a warning or qualification: as for example in d'Anglebert's *Gavottes* (*cf.* vol. 1, p. 44), where the word *lentement* (*slowly*) does not mean that the piece should sound slow, but that the normal beat for a *Gavotte* here applies to the quaver instead of the more usual crotchet or minim.

The familiar Italian tempo marks also began life as descriptions of mood, for the literal meaning of *Allegro* is 'cheerful', while *Adagio* means 'gently, at ease'; but by the mid-18th century they had already acquired most of the meanings we know today. J. J. Quantz in 1752 relates tempi to pulse-beats, like Mersenne and Simpson a hundred years earlier, and gives definitions which in terms of the metronome may be tabulated thus:

Speeds given by Quantz, 1752, for
Italian tempo-marks in Common-time

Presto, Allegro assai	♩ = 160
Vivace, Allegro, Allegro moderato	♩ = 120
Allegretto	♩ = 80
Adagio cantabile	♪ = 80
Adagio assai	♪ = 40

Like the earlier definitions, these will be found too restricted in practice; nevertheless, they are interesting from a comparative point of view and as very rough approximations.

The established dance-forms used by so many of the early keyboard composers also provide useful indications of tempi, for descriptions of them can be found in several contemporary treatises. We read in Thomas Morley's fascinating *A Plaine and Easie Introduction to Practicall Musicke*, 1597 (modern reprint ed. R. Alec Harman: Dent, London 1952), that the *Pavan* is 'a kind of staid music ordained for grave dancing'; and that 'after every Pavan we usually set a *Galliarde*, a lighter and more stirring kind of dancing'. 'The Alman', Morley adds, 'is a more heavy dance than this', while the *Branle Double* is quicker. 'Like unto this (but more light) be the *Voltes* and *Courantes* [*Corantos*] which . . . are danced after sundry fashions, the Volte rising and leaping, the Courante travising [traversing] and running'.

A hundred years later several French theorists began to measure dance tempi with primitive types of metronomes. From the writings of Michel L'Affilard (1694), L. L. Pajot (1732), J. A. La Chapelle (1737) and H. L. Choquel (1759) we may deduce the following speeds for some of the more important dances of the period:

	MM	
Allemande	120	for each of 2 beats per bar
Courante	82–90	3
Gavotte	98–152	2
Gigue	104–120	2
Menuet	70–80	1
Rigaudon	116–152	2
Sarabande	63–80	3
Tambourin	176	2

Two points about this table must, however, be remembered. Firstly, the notation of the French harpsichordists often requires the beat to apply not to half-bars (minims) but to crotchets, and sometimes even to quavers as we have seen from the *Gavottes* of d'Anglebert. And secondly, the tempi were judged by the straightforward dances of the stage or ballroom, and therefore sometimes require to be slower for the richly elaborated movements of the harpsichordists. Generally speaking, it will be found that the beat remains more or less within the limits shown for the *Allemande, Courante, Gavotte* and *Sarabande*, though not necessarily the number of beats per bar; while for the *Rigaudon* and *Tambourin* it will have to be somewhat slower, and for the *Gigue* and *Menuet* considerably slower.

It is also useful to remember that the tempo of dance movements tends to slow down over the years. For example, the Sarabande was quick enough in Purcell's day to make a satisfactory finish to a Suite, whereas for Bach it was essentially a slow movement.

With all questions of tempo the player must take into consideration the prevailing texture and movement of the music. A piece that is full of demi-semiquavers or very complicated ornamentation, or one that has harmonic shifts on every quaver, is likely to require a comparatively slow crotchet; while a piece that has no note smaller than a quaver, little ornamentation, and a change of harmony only once every minim, will need a crotchet that is comparatively quick. All such relevant factors must be weighed together and balanced with what is known or may be deduced of the form, character and mood of the

---

† This was clearly a misprint for ◑.

piece concerned. Then, by trial and error and continual adjustment, the player must gradually find his way towards the tempo that he feels will express most satisfactorily the inherent qualities of the music.

With regard to consistency of tempo within a single movement: Couperin gives two useful hints in *L'Art de Toucher le Clavecin*, 1717. At one point he writes, 'Take great care not to alter the tempo in a measured piece'; and at another, 'A Prelude is a free composition . . . [and should be played] in a free style without sticking too closely to the tempo, unless I have shown otherwise by the word *Mesuré*'. In fact, as Couperin implies, the important point is the *type* of music concerned. In the freer forms, such as Toccatas, improvisatory Preludes and the like, the tempo must also be free; while in stricter, more self-contained forms, such as dances and fugues, the tempo should be strict. Borderline cases will always exist, and there the player must use his common sense. Some of the long sets of virginalist variations, for example, contain such a wide range of note-values that it is impossible to find a tempo that will fit every variation equally satisfactorily. This in itself is a proof that the composer intended the basic tempo to be altered as occasion demanded, as, indeed, Frescobaldi recommends in the preface to his Toccatas of 1614-15 (*cf. Italy: Ornamentation*, vol. 2, p. 11).

Phrasing and Articulation

Problems of phrasing and articulation might at first sight seem less important than those of tempo; yet, if anything, the reverse is true. Phrasing, though so rarely marked in early scores, is the breath and life of music, and a performance that lacks it is as meaningless as unpunctuated speech. It is therefore essential for a player to learn to phrase and articulate an unmarked score idiomatically.

As the terms are so often loosely used, it may be as well to begin with three definitions. In the following discussion a *phrase* is taken to be a natural musical division comparable to a sentence of speech; hence *phrasing* is concerned with showing these divisions, both short and long, and their relationship one with another. *Articulation*, on the other hand, is a subsidiary of phrasing, and is concerned with whether a note is joined to its neighbour or neighbours, or is in some degree detached.

PHRASING

Musical phrases, like spoken sentences, are defined by being separated from one another by 'breaths' of varying length, corresponding roughly to the effect of commas, semi-colons and full-stops, etc. These minute silences are made, generally without disturbing the time-scheme, by shortening the last note of a phrase; but when a more marked break is required, it may be also necessary occasionally—particularly in more romantic types of music—to lengthen the bar by a fraction, or even to make a tiny *rit*. Such breaks are infinitesimal, and much of the art of phrasing lies in the subtlety with which they are differentiated and executed.

To discover the phrasing of an unmarked and unfamiliar work, the student should begin by reading it through as best he may. He should then turn back to the beginning and play as far as the first obvious halting place, such as a specially strong cadence, a cadence preceding a new musical idea, or a double bar. Having established this initial paragraph, he should then proceed to break it down into its constituent sections and phrases, which he will find are generally rounded off by cadences of varying strength. Finally, with these musical divisions clearly in his head, or marked in pencil on the score, he should ask himself two questions: (a) which are the more important and which are the less important breaks between phrases? and (b) where is the climax of the whole paragraph?—that is, the point towards which the tension mounts and away from which it slackens.

Having analyzed the first paragraph in this way, he should pass on to the second and treat it similarly. And so on with the rest of the work; always relating each new paragraph to those that have gone before, so that the whole is kept in correct perspective and the main climax of the work is clearly differentiated from the less important climaxes.

As an example of this approach it may be helpful to consider for a moment the Byrd *Galiardo* on p. 25. After reading the piece through, without bothering about ornamentation or minor details, the student would start again at the beginning and play probably to the end of b.8, where there is both a strong cadence and a double bar. On returning once more to the beginning, he would find that this initial paragraph is made up of the following three phrases:

    1. b.1 to the 3rd beat of b.4
    2. 4th beat of b.4 to the 3rd beat of b.6
    3. 4th beat of b.6 to the end of b.8

Considering their relationship, he would find that the most important break (the equivalent of a full-stop) comes at the end of the third; that there is a less important break (a semi-colon) at the end of the first; and a still less important one (a comma) at the end of the second. He would also find that the climax of the paragraph coincides with the melodic climax on the 3rd crotchet of b.7.

Having established the shape of this first paragraph, the student would then pass on to the second—which also happens to be the last—and analyze it similarly. (It contains three phrases: 1. b.9 to the 3rd beat of b.12; 2. 4th beat of b.12 to the 3rd beat of b.13; 3. 4th beat of b.13 to the end of b.16.) Here however he would find that the climax is harmonic rather than melodic. It occurs on the 1st beat of b.15; and since it is more intense than that of the previous paragraph, it also forms the climax of the whole piece.

Phrase-analysis of this kind not only shows the performer where the music 'breathes', it also provides him with a key to one of the most important forms of contrast available to a composer: the use of varying phrase-lengths. At first sight Byrd's *Galiardo* might seem rather a square little piece consisting of sixteen bars divided into two equal halves. Yet analysis shows—and the player must make this clear to the listener—that it is far from square, since it is made up of the following unexpected sequence of bars: $3\frac{1}{2}$, 2, $2\frac{1}{2}$: $3\frac{1}{2}$, 1, $3\frac{1}{2}$.

The student must also be on the look out for the less straightforward types of phrase that overlap and dovetail.

Overlapping phrases occur most frequently between different voices in contrapuntal textures, where the entries of the voices are usually 'staggered' to a greater or lesser degree. Examples can be found in bb.5-8 of the same Byrd *Galiardo*, where the l.h. echoes the r.h. at the distance of a bar. Such overlaps are characteristic of all contrapuntal music, whether imitation is present or not; so much so, indeed, that the student should always question his phrasing of counterpoint if he finds, at points other than cadences, that phrases in different voices end simultaneously.

In *Dovetailed phrases* a single note provides both the end of one phrase and the beginning of the next. There are several in the Purcell *Prelude* on p. 36: e.g. the first r.h. semiquaver D in b.11, and the first r.h. B flat in b.20. Such joins sometimes require a fraction of extra time in performance—as for example at the end of b.10 of the *Prelude*, where the structurally important cadence will sound perfunctory if played strictly in time.

ARTICULATION

Once the length of a phrase has been found, the next thing to decide is how it should be articulated: i.e. which of its notes shall be separated (and to what extent), and which joined to its neighbour or neighbours.

From surviving examples of early keyboard fingering it is clear that the music of the 16th, 17th and early 18th centuries was broken up in performance into much smaller units than is customary with late 18th and 19th century music. Players originally relied mainly on the middle three fingers of each hand, passing the long 3rd finger over the 4th in r.h. ascending scales and over the 2nd in descending ones (vice versa in the l.h.), and the 5th finger and thumb were used far less frequently than in present-day fingering. (For examples of early fingering *cf.* Couperin's *Les Ondes*, p. 49, and the *Suggestions for Further Reading*, p. 20, under Couperin, Dolmetsch and Matchett.) As a result, music was generally less smoothly articulated than it would be today—though of course a grave or stately mood would have called for more sustained treatment, e.g. in the Byrd *Pavana*, p. 24, or the Gibbons *Fantazia*, p. 30.

The type of broken articulation required by much early music can be seen from the Byrd *Galiardo* already mentioned. If its first half were played legato, as is perfectly possible with modern fingering, it would sound airless, flat and dull. But when its opening phrase is articulated

in some such way as ♩. ♫ ♩ ♩ , the dance-like charac-

ter of the piece immediately becomes apparent, and the lively imitation between the voices stands out clearly instead of being wrapped in fog.

This 'characterization' of themes is one of the most important functions of articulation in the performance of early music, for it brings out their inherent life and enables the most involved contrapuntal textures to remain transparent. Another of its functions is to define the smaller units out of which passage-work is built.

Long legato stretches of quickly moving notes, so characteristic of 19th century composers such as Chopin and Liszt, are foreign to harpsichord music and reduce it to the level of a Czerny exercise. For an idiomatic performance, the player must always be aware of the smaller patterns that underlie the figuration, and aim to show these by means of subtle articulation, while preserving at the same time the all-important overall line. Indeed, to be aware of the sub-divisions is almost sufficient, for if they are in any way over-emphasized the long line will disappear.

In Farnaby's *Tell mee Daphne* on p. 28, for example, the semiquavers in bb.9-10 must be felt to consist of four-note groups, beginning on the second semiquaver of each beat. The unbroken line of the first half of b.11 then comes as a welcome contrast, followed by the unexpected break in the second half of the bar between the two l.h. Ds. Upbeat articulation is resumed in b.12, first of all in groups of eight semiquavers and then in groups of four, and is continued until the end of strain 2, apart from a further refreshing contrast of four pairs of semiquavers in the first half of b.15.

In order to make such subtleties of articulation clear, it is almost always necessary to play quickly-moving early music at a noticeably slower tempo than would be natural to passage-work of the 19th century. The notes must be allowed time to breathe and establish their individuality, as it were, and must never be herded into anonymous groups. This rule applies equally strongly to the music of baroque composers such as Couperin and Bach, even though an increasing use of the thumb and fifth finger was beginning to bring greater speeds within the player's reach, as can be seen from some of the startlingly brilliant Sonatas of Scarlatti. (The old and new systems of fingering are shown side by side in C. P. E. Bach's *Essay on the True Art of Keyboard Playing*, 1753.)

But even when the fundamental importance of articulation is recognized and accepted, the student is still faced with the problem of how he shall decide its details.

Perhaps the best approach to finding the articulation of a phrase in an unmarked score is to sing, hum, or whistle it. This may not provide the final answer; but it leads in the right direction, for it shows the melodic contour, the climax of the phrase, the notes that form indivisible musical groups, and the places where natural breaks occur. Next the student might imagine how the phrase would be bowed by a string player, and in particular just how detached each individual non-legato note would be. He should then think of the harmonic aspect, and make sure that both the basic harmony and the progressions underlying the melodic decoration are supported and not contradicted by the articulation. For example, in the Blow *Gavott* on p. 35, the r.h. part taken by itself might suggest that a new sub-phrase begins on the 4th beat E of b.2; yet a glance at the bass shows that in fact the E belongs to the preceding F since it supplies its resolution, and that therefore the two notes must be slurred together.

By analogy with vocal music it will often be found that stepwise movement suggests legato, particularly if the steps are chromatic; while jumps (other than arpeggios, which are often merely broken chords) suggest staccato. Hence a leap interrupting stepwise movement is likely to imply a break in legato. This is of course only the roughest of generalizations, which is often invalidated by other considerations.

True syncopations—that is, misplaced accents and not simply resolutions of appoggiaturas—can generally be treated fairly consistently. As one of the clearest ways to accent a note (the only way, indeed, on the organ) is to shorten the one before it, the note preceding a syncopation usually tends to be more or less staccato.

Two slightly misleading types of notation, both concerned with articulation, must be remembered by the student. In one, a single line is written as though it were in two parts; in the other, on the contrary, two sustained parts are written as though they were a single line. In Bach's F minor Prelude from Book I of the '48' the r.h. is notated thus:

But this does not mean, as it would in later piano music, that the notes with crotchet stems should be made to stand out as a separate melodic part. A moment's experiment on a harpsichord will show that the melody is contained in the semiquaver line, and that the crotchets are held down merely to enrich the harmonic background. The same notation is also used occasionally to show that all the notes relevant to the harmony should be sustained, and not only those that are marked. (*cf.* the Introduction to Vol. 2, p. 10, under *Germany: Ornamentation* [*17*] *Arpeggio*.)

Almost the opposite situation is found in passages such as the following from the *Allemande* of Bach's French Suite IV in E flat:

Here a contemporary performer would almost certainly have played *molto tenuto*, as a contrast to the true single line of the r.h. in the preceding 2½ bars:

And a more meticulous composer would have notated it thus, as can be seen from bb.9-10 of Couperin's *La Convalescente*, on p. 46.

No hard and fast rules about such passages can, however, be made. Like all questions of articulation, each depends on its context; and each must finally rely for its solution on the musical instinct of the player.

FURTHER HINTS ON PHRASING AND ARTICULATION

1. An excess of legato in performance produces opaque stodginess, and too much staccato makes for a restless lack of continuity. Some pieces demand more legato and less staccato than others, and vice versa; but on the whole the two should be fairly evenly balanced.

2. Look out for patterns of figuration and of phrase-length, and note particularly where they change.

3. Figurative patterns that match should have matching articulation: those that differ should have differing articulation.

4. 'Characterize' fugue subjects, counter-subjects and episodes with suitably contrasted articulation, so that they may preserve their identity.

5. In pre-classical music, up-beat phrasing is more usual than on-the-beat phrasing. When a piece or a paragraph begins with an up-beat, the phrasing thereafter tends to do likewise: e.g. in the Bull *Gigge*, p. 26, and in the pieces by Couperin, Dandrieu and Daquin.

6. Since a cadence = repose, and a climax = tension, the climax of a paragraph is almost certain to be a chord other than the prevailing tonic.

7. A dissonance or suspension should not be separated from its resolution. There is, however, an exception to this rule. If the resolution is ornamental, with one or more notes interposed between it and the discord, a new phrase often begins on the first note of the ornamental resolution.

Dynamics

Dynamic markings are rare in music before the mid-17th century; but this does not mean that earlier composers wished their works to be performed at a single dull dynamic level. Dynamic inflection is inherent in vocal music, since it is difficult to avoid singing a high note more loudly than a low one; it seems likely, therefore, that this natural effect was always recognized by composers, and accepted as a normal part of all music, instrumental as well as vocal.

For present purposes we may divide dynamics into two types: (a) inflectional dynamics, which may best be compared to the rise and fall of a speaking voice; and (b) structural dynamics, which (to continue the analogy) mirror the contrast between a single voice and the combined voices of a crowd. The two types are not mutually exclusive: they overlap continually, and both are fundamental to music.

Among old keyboard instruments the clavichord is ideally fitted to reproduce inflectional dynamics (see p. 7, *Tonal Characteristics of the older instruments*); and though the harpsichord can only hint at these, it is perfectly adapted to the display of structural dynamics by reason of the clear-cut contrast between its two manuals. When performing old music on the piano, it is important to bear both these instrumental characteristics in mind.

To determine inflectional dynamics it will generally be found helpful to think of the music in terms of the voice. The melodic rise and fall tends to be echoed by a dynamic rise and fall; and though this must at times give way to other considerations, it usually provides a useful starting point. The phrasing is also an important factor: for the shape of a phrase conditions its dynamics, and dynamics help to define the phrase. Hence it is important for the player to decide where the climax of a phrase occurs—it may or may not coincide with the melodic peak—and what relationship it bears to neighbouring phrases. (*cf.* the Note on Gibbons' *Fantazia*, vol. 1, p. 30.) The harmony must also be considered. Discord implies tension and hence accent, while concord implies relaxation and lack of accent; thus a cadence, as its name suggests, generally requires a dynamic fall.

The keyboard layout used by an idiomatic harpsichord composer such as Scarlatti often incorporates its own dynamics. The texture will be thinned out in order to tail-off a phrase; or, on the contrary, a thick chord will be introduced when an accent is required. On the harpsichord these changes in texture automatically produce the effect required; but the pianist must learn to recognize them when he sees them on the printed page, so that in performance he may reproduce them clearly in terms of pianistic dynamics.

Generally speaking, inflectional dynamics in early music operate on a more restricted scale than in the works of Classical and Romantic composers. The sort of dramatic contrasts and changes that are natural to Beethoven would usually be out of place in Byrd, Couperin or Bach—though a surprisingly wide range is covered by some of Bach's Toccatas and Fantasies, and similar works. But a subtle degree of dynamic fluctuation is always inherent in the music, and to ignore this is to reduce a performance to the level of typewriting.

The most important example of structural dynamics in keyboard music is the use of the two manuals of a harpsichord to reproduce the tutti and solo elements in Ritornello or Concerto form, which forms the basis of so many of Bach's large-scale instrumental and vocal works. This practice was so well understood by contemporaries that the necessary changes of manual are often left unmarked in the score. In such cases we must supply them for ourselves, if we are going to understand the structure of the movement concerned and make it clear to listeners. (*cf.* the *Prelude* to Bach's English Suite in A minor, vol. 2, p. 22.)

Fortunately Bach himself indicated the necessary manual-changes in several of his works, such as the *Italian Concerto* for solo harpsichord, whose first movement is so fully marked that it can be used as a pattern for every movement of this type. The words *forte* and *piano* here stand for the two contrasting manuals of the instrument. A *forte* in both hands represents a tutti; while a solo passage is shown either by a *forte* in one hand and a *piano* in the other, or by a *piano* in both. (The unmarked opening is understood, as usual, to be *forte*.) The structure revealed is that of the normal baroque Concerto, in which identical tutti paragraphs open and close a movement, and act as a frame to alternating appearances of the solo and tutti.

When transferring this effect to the piano it must be remembered that the essential contrast is between tutti and solo, rather than between *forte* and *piano*. That is to say, the two-handed *forte* of a tutti passage must be differentiated from the single-handed *forte* of a solo; for on a harpsichord the latter, in combination with the *piano* of the remaining hand, would in fact produce the effect of a *mezzo-forte*. If this distinction is not made, the contrast between solo and tutti is obscured and the whole structure endangered. It should be remembered, too, that on the piano inflectional dynamics are required within the broader contrasts of solo and tutti.

Another use of structural dynamics is to underline the contrast between different sections of large-scale works such as Toccatas. The more brilliant and rhetorical sections would be played on one manual and the more reflective ones on the other; and this broad contrast should be made clear when such works are transferred to the piano.

The two manuals of a harpsichord can also be used purely for effects of colour. Thus the single *forte* and *piano* at the beginning of the slow movement of the *Italian Concerto* have no structural purpose, but merely show that the right hand is the solo and the left hand the accompaniment throughout. A pianist would produce this effect almost without thinking, for it is suggested by the very texture of the music.

Another common use of the two contrasting manuals is to obtain echo effects. These are often intended by the composer, even when unmarked; but the pianist should beware of introducing them indiscriminately, whenever he happens to find a phrase that is exactly repeated, for they can very easily make the music sound irritatingly short-winded. (*cf.* the Arne *Gigue*, vol. 1, p. 40.)

Fingering

As we have already seen, it can be a great help in determining articulation to have some knowledge of early keyboard fingering, which relied mainly on the middle three fingers of each hand. It would be unpractical, however, to limit ourselves to its use in performance today, for not only is it less suited to the heavy touch of modern instruments, but it would necessitate unlearning our present system in which the five digits are of equal importance. Nor is it necessary to do this, so long as we are careful to reproduce in our phrasing all the essential musical implications of the older system.

One of the principal aims of good fingering is to avoid unnecessary hand movement. Hence it is often helpful to see how many notes of a phrase can be played legato without any hand-shift. If the whole phrase can be included, the student should then decide whether this fingering will best produce the articulation he requires, or whether it would be clearer with a less static hand position. For example, the following passage can be played without a hand-shift by using the fingering shown above the stave: ; yet the articulation might be clearer and more precise if one of the lower fingerings were used instead, though all of these involve hand movement. In every instance the student must weigh up the various alternatives, and decide which one will best achieve the musical effect he is aiming at.

When shifts are necessary, they should if possible be made to underline the phrasing rather than contradict it; thus it is always an advantage if hand-shifts can be made to coincide with breaks in a phrase.

In passage-work the student should continually be on the look-out for patterns in the music—particularly the less obvious ones that begin off the beat—and should try to match them with fingering patterns. For example, the following left-hand passage from Bach's *Fugue on a theme by Albinoni* (vol. 2, p. 34) looks at first sight rather awkward:

but it is perfectly easy both to finger and to play as soon as it is realized that it consists of three phrases, as shown by the square brackets, each beginning on the second semiquaver of a four-note group, and each fingered 1243.

In passages founded on broken chords it is always a good plan to begin by reducing the chords to their unbroken form, as they will then show plainly where the most natural hand-shifts occur.

In contrapuntal music and music that is mainly legato it is frequently necessary to revert to the old practice of crossing a long finger over a shorter one, thus:

the longer finger being used wherever possible on a black note.

A change of finger on a single note can be used for two precisely opposite effects: (a) to underline detached phrasing, as shown in the first example above; and (b) to obtain a long legato. Couperin's example of a legato is given below, with his own fingering shown above the stave and the more usual modern fingering underneath:

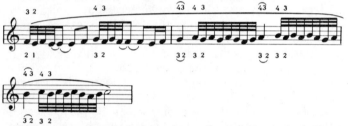

When the detailed fingering of a passage has been worked out, its essential features should be written into the copy; but everything that is obvious or can be taken for granted should be omitted. Changes of hand position are important, and can generally be made clear for the right hand by marking the thumbs in ascending passages, and the third and fourth fingers in descending ones; and vice versa for the left hand. Any unexpected or irregular fingerings should also be marked, preferably only by means of the key fingers involved. Otherwise the student's aim should be to reduce the fingering in his copy to the minimum consistent with clarity, for the fewer the marks the easier they are to read.

Piano Pedalling

Since early keyboard instruments had no sustaining pedal, it is essential to avoid the anachronistic use of the pedal when playing old music on the piano. The sustaining pedal can provide an invaluable extension of the piano's range of colour; but in doing so it must never be allowed to produce the sort of effect that belongs exclusively to a later type of music. For example, if the figure

appeared in the left hand part of a piece of 19th century piano music, it is more than likely that the composer would have intended all five notes to be held throughout the bar by means of the pedal. A harpsichord composer, on the other hand, would never have intended such an effect, for the simple reason that it was impossible on the instrument for which he was writing.

He might have played anything between

and ; but with a single hand he could not possibly have sustained the first three quavers into the second half of the bar. Hence it would be a mistake to use the pedal to do so on the piano, should we meet such a passage in a harpsichord or clavichord work. (See the Scarlatti Sonata in F minor, vol. 2, p. 58.)

The safest way to find the proper use of the sustaining pedal in old music is to begin by playing a piece without any pedal at all. (The possibilities of the *tenuto* type of touch shown in the third example above should never be forgotten, for it is a most important resource in harpsichord and clavichord playing.) Having achieved the phrasing that the music demands, the player can then add any touches of pedal that may be required for purposes of colour, being careful neither to obscure nor contradict the phrasing he has already obtained. If he does this with care, he may be surprised at the number of pedal changes that are required—one on every semiquaver is by no means unusual; but he will be well on the way to mastering the type of pedalling that can be used without anachronism in the performance of old music.

The left-hand ('soft') pedal is less of a problem. Since it effects nothing but the tone, it can be used for long or short periods as required. The player must, however, be on his guard against relying on its help every time he wants to produce a quiet sound; otherwise he will inevitably halve the number of colours at his disposal, and (worse still) become incapable of appreciating and producing subtle tonal differences by the use of his fingers alone.

England: Ornamentation

The English virginalist composers used two principal ornaments: a single oblique line drawn above the note, below it, or through its stem; and a pair of oblique lines similarly placed. Surprisingly enough, no contemporary writer refers to these ornaments, so their interpretation remains uncertain; it seems likely, however, that it depends largely on context. The single-stroke ornament may imply either a slide from a 3rd below, or a lower *appoggiatura;* while the more common double-stroke probably stands for a shake of some sort—either long or short, with upper or lower auxiliary, and starting on either the main note or the upper auxiliary, but generally without a termination—or even for a short, upper or lower *appoggiatura.*

Suggested realizations of these ornaments are given above or below the stave of the virginal pieces in this volume, but they must not be taken as definitive: they merely show possible solutions of the problem. For example, the editor often interprets as in a descending phrase and as in an ascending one; yet this practice is only based on the fact that it is more natural for the fingers to play an auxiliary note in the direction from which the phrase approaches the ornament.

The main function of ornamentation in virginal music appears to be to supply accent; but its use is singularly haphazard, and different manuscripts of the same piece rarely agree on the subject. This suggests that the virginalists regarded ornaments less as an integral part of the music than as a pleasing embellishment to be added or omitted according to taste. For this reason we may feel justified, when transferring the music to the piano, in treating the ornaments with some freedom; particularly as their effect is so different on the two instruments, and the piano can in any case provide accents by other means. On the virginals they add a delightful sparkle and zest to the music, whereas on the piano they tend, unless played with great skill, ease and lightness, to make the texture sound thick and over-crowded. This is not always so, of course. Often the full ornamentation can be played quite satisfactorily on the piano; but at times it may be advisable to omit some or even all of it. The virginalist ornaments, like most others, should be played on the beat.

By the end of the 17th century more definite information is available concerning ornamentation. For example, there are 'Rules for Graces' in Purcell's *A Choice Collection of Lessons*, 1696; and though they contain serious misprints, there is no reason to suppose that they fundamentally misrepresent contemporary practice. The following list gives the gist of the rules with their inaccuracies corrected:

Corrected table of Ornaments from Purcell's 'A Choice Collection of Lessons', 1696

It has always been obvious that the Battery's original explanation was badly garbled. But no one seems to have accounted hitherto for the equally odd original explanation of the Beat: .

Yet if we look at Purcell's use of the ornament in his Suites it becomes clear that this explanation really applies to a *Forefall and beat;* and that the name and sign for the latter, together with the correct explanation of the Beat, have been left out of the original engraving by mistake. The missing signs and words have been added in square

brackets to the above table, which gives the list of ornaments as it should stand.

Note that the sign ᴍ has here just the reverse of its usual meaning: that is to say, for Purcell and his English contemporaries it means the same as the normal sign ᴡ.

By the middle of the 18th century English composers had abandoned the older signs in favour of those in more general use. In Arne's Sonatas of 1756 we find both ᴡ and *tr* standing for a shake (always beginning on the note above), ∿ for , and the customary ᴡ for .

Small notes are also used singly and in groups. The majority should be played, like the other ornaments, on the beat; but an exception should be made with the small notes that terminate a shake, and also probably with the four-note group found in the first movement of Sonata No. 5.

England: Repeat Signs

The virginalists, like some later composers, rarely used repeat signs. They relied on the player to make the repeats required, and also to adjust the text if necessary so that the final bar of a strain would serve as both 1st- and 2nd-time bar. When this has not already been done by the editor, the student must be prepared to do it for himself; he should therefore remember the following facts:

1. In virginal music it was usual to repeat each strain of a dance movement, unless the piece already included written-out divisions (that is, varied repeats).

2. The virginalists often repeated short dance movements *in toto;* so it is in order to do this when the player feels a piece is on the short side.

3. Generally speaking, other repeats are unnecessary; but each individual case must be judged in its musical context.

England: Peculiarities of the Fitzwilliam Virginal Book

As the Fitzwilliam Virginal Book is the most important extant source of early English keyboard music, it is worth remembering certain peculiarities of its notation. These are fully discussed in the present writer's article 'Repeats and Final Bars in the Fitzwilliam Virginal Book', *Music and Letters*, Vol. 43, No. 4, Oct., 1962; but here they may be briefly summarized thus:

1. Repeats in the Fitzwilliam Virginal Book should be governed by the rules given above and not by the repeat-marks in the complete printed edition, which only represent an ornamental feature of the original copyist's calligraphy.

2. The many final breve bars that are found in the Fitzwilliam Book fall into two classes: (a) those that resolve the melody or harmony, or complete the expected rhythmic scheme; and (b) the remainder, which are musically redundant. Those in class (a) should of course always be played; but those in class (b) should be omitted in performance, as they were only another ornamental feature of the copyist's calligraphy. (See Bull's *Gigge* and Farnaby's *Tell mee Daphne*, pp. 26 & 28.)

Tregian, the copyist of the Fitzwilliam Book, generally numbered the strains or other sections of a piece, and often marked the divisions (varied repeats) with the sign *Rep.* These indications are helpful to the performer, so they have been added here when necessary.

France: Ornamentation

Ornamentation plays a more essential part in French harpsichord music than in the music of the English virginalists, so it should not be omitted even on the piano. Most of the outstanding French composers included tables of ornaments with their published pieces; for, as C. P. E. Bach wrote in 1753, 'they notate their ornaments with painstaking accuracy'. The composers agree fairly well among themselves over their explanations of ornaments, except for a few minor details and the names they use; unfortunately they are not so unanimous in

COMPARATIVE TABLE OF FRENC

their use of signs. These can best be understood by a glance at the table printed below, which includes all the French ornaments found in this volume. The usual name for each ornament is given in the left hand column; this is followed by the modern sign (if one exists) and explanation, together with the sign and explanation given by Chambonnières, d'Anglebert, François Couperin, Rameau and Dandrieu. The name used for any ornament by an individual composer is only given if it differs from that shown in the left hand column.

RNAMENTS USED IN THIS VOLUME

Several points concerning these ornaments should be noted:

1. They should all be played on the beat.

2. It is quite possible that Chambonnières' explanation of No. 1, the *Port de voix*, is a misprint, as a repeated note within an ornament is most unusual at this period. It seems very likely that the explanation should read [musical figure], to conform with that given by Chambonnières' own pupil d'Anglebert.

3. It is surprising that Couperin should give the name *Port de voix simple* to No. 4, which would be more logically called a *Port de voix et pincé*. However, Couperin's name may not be a misprint, as Daquin in a note prefacing his *Pièces* of 1735 calls the following a *Port de voix:* [musical figure] .Incidentally, Daquin's realization of the ornament, with its delayed attack, is an interesting example of what Couperin calls a *Suspension*, noted and explained [musical figure] .

4. Another puzzling piece of terminology is the use of two signs and two names, the *Tremblement lié* and the *Tremblement appuyé* (Nos. 6 & 7) for apparently the same effect. J. S. Bach also has two signs for this ornament (see Introduction to vol. 2); but at least he uses the same name (*accent und trillo*) and explanation for each.

5. It is easy to confuse Chambonnières' and Couperin's signs for upward and downward arpeggios. Remember that in all four the hook is printed near the note on which the arpeggio starts. In the signs used by d'Anglebert and Rameau the slope of the oblique line shows the direction in which the arpeggio moves.

In spite of C. P. E. Bach's remark about the 'painstaking accuracy' of French ornamentation, the composers' tables are often far from clear about the duration of an ornament. Even Couperin in his *L'Art de Toucher le Clavecin* is not always explicit, though the following rules can be gleaned from what he writes:

1. The duration of an ornament such as a *Pincé-double* (with or without *Port de voix*) and a *Tremblement* is determined by the value of the note above which it is written. (He does not define the length of the *Port de voix* itself. D'Anglebert and Rameau show it as taking half the length of the main note; but in some contexts it is necessary to make it shorter.)

2. A *Pincé-double* has two components: (a) the *battements* or repercussions, and (b) the *point-d'arrêt* or stopping place. The *battements* begin on the beat, continue for (probably) half the value of the note, then stop on the *point-d'arrêt*, that is, the note itself. Thus [musical figure] would be played either [musical figure] or [musical figure] , depending on the speed of the piece.

3. A *Tremblement* has three components: (a) the *appui* or preparation, (b) the *battements*, and (c) the *point-d'arrêt*. The *appui* comes on the beat, and consists of a dwelling on the note above the main note; and the two remaining components follow. (Couperin's notation is

[musical figure with *tremblement* and labels (a) (b) (c)] ; but here he seems to be describing a *Tremblement appuyé* rather than a plain *Tremblement*. As with some other of his explanations, it looks as though he has mixed up his terms.)

4. If a *Tremblement* occurs on a short note, the *point-d'arrêt*, or both *appui* and *point-d'arrêt* may be omitted.

5. Sometimes a *Tremblement* should be played *aspiré:* that is, cut short by a rest.

6. A *Tremblement* should begin more slowly than it ends.

Concerning ornamentation in general, Couperin gives an invaluable hint that may be applied to that of every school and period. He writes that ornaments should be practised very slowly to begin with. If this is done consistently, and the rhythm clearly defined from the start, it will be found that they soon become an integral part of the music, instead of sounding like awkward excrescences.

France: Notes inégales

Elsewhere in *L'Art de Toucher le Clavecin* Couperin refers to an important French rhythmic convention which is too often ignored in performance today. He writes:

> We [the French] write music differently from the way we play it; which is why foreigners play our music less well than we play theirs. The Italians, on the contrary, write their music with the true time-values, as they wish it played.

Here Couperin is speaking of *Notes inégales*, a type of rhythmic freedom or rubato used under certain conditions in French music to intensify either its grace and charm or, on the contrary, its rhythmic vigour. Briefly it consists in altering the time-values of certain *pairs* of notes (never triplets). The alterations are of three kinds: (a) *lourer,* the most common, in which for example [musical figure] would become [musical figure] or [musical figure] ; (b) *couler,* in which [musical figure] becomes [musical figure] ; and (c) *pointer* or *piquer,* in which [musical figure] becomes [musical figure] .

The rules for the use of these different types of *notes inégales* may be summed up as follows:

1. *LOURER*

When the time-signature is	pairs of notes in these time-values should generally be played long-short.
$\frac{3}{1}$	[half–half]
$\frac{3}{2}$	[half–half] and [quarter-pair figure]
2, ¢ (as 2 in a bar), 3, $\frac{3}{4}, \frac{6}{4}, \frac{9}{4}, \frac{12}{4}$	[quarter-pair figure]
4, C, ¢ (as 4 in a bar), $\frac{4}{4}, \frac{2}{4}, \frac{3}{8}, \frac{4}{8}, \frac{6}{8}, \frac{9}{8}, \frac{12}{8}$	[eighth-pair figure]
$\frac{3}{16}, \frac{4}{16}, \frac{6}{16}, \frac{9}{16}, \frac{12}{16}$	[sixteenth-pair figure]

Exceptions: notes inégales are not used

(a) in passages of disjunct movement featuring harmony rather than melody;

(b) when a piece is headed *Notes égales, martelées, détachées, mouvement décidé* or *marqué;*

(c) when the notes are syncopated, or mixed up with rests;

(d) when they are merely repetitions of a single note;

(e) when they have dots, dashes or lines written above them, thus: ♪♪ , ♪♪ or ♪♪ . (N.B. in French music of this period a staccato is implied by ♪ but *not* by ♪);

(f) when more than a single pair of notes are slurred together;

(g) when a pair of notes is marked ♩♩ or ♩♩ (see under *Couler* below);

(h) in very quick movements (here the first of every group of four notes may be lengthened, or all may be played evenly: see Daquin's *L'Hirondelle* in the present volume); and

(i) in vigorous or deliberately four-square movements where grace and charm would be out of keeping (see Rameau's *La Triomphante* in the present volume).

2. *COULER*

If a pair of notes is written with a slur and a dot ♩♩ , or ♫ , the rhythm should be altered to short-long ♫ .

3. *POINTER or PIQUER*

If a pair of notes with the written rhythm ♩.♪ appears in a context where an undotted pair ♫ would be played *louré*, the first pair should be played as though it were double-dotted ♩..♪ . (See Dandrieu's *La Lyre d'Orphée* in the present volume, where the double-dotting applies to dotted-crotchet-and-quaver pairs.)

No hard and fast rules can be given for the degree of unevenness required by any of these *notes inégales*. Indeed, their whole point is that they should mean slightly different things at different times. The evidence of contemporary musical-boxes shows, however, that the unevenness ranged from $\frac{3}{4}$ plus $\frac{1}{4}$ (that is, exactly ♩.♪) to $\frac{7}{12}$ plus $\frac{5}{12}$ (which is almost ♫); and with this as a guide, the student must decide for himself exactly what is required by the character of the music in each instance. In doing so, he will not only be refining his rhythmic perception and musicianship, but also cultivating that *bon goût* which the French masters deemed so essential to the proper performance of their music.

SUGGESTIONS FOR FURTHER READING

C. P. E. Bach, *Versuch über die wahre Art das Klavier zu spielen*, 1753; (English translation by WILLIAM J. MITCHELL, *Essay on the True Art of Playing Keyboard Instruments:* Cassell, London 1949).

J. S. Bach, *48 Preludes & Fugues*, ed. with a Preface & Notes by DONALD FRANCIS TOVEY: Associated Board, London 1924.

J. S. Bach, *The 'Goldberg' Variations*, ed. with a Preface by RALPH KIRKPATRICK: Schirmer, New York 1938.

Eugéne Borrel, *L'Interprétation de la Musique Française:* Alcan, Paris 1934.

Charles van den Borren, *The Sources of Keyboard Music in England:* Novello, London 1913.

François Couperin, *L'Art de Toucher le Clavecin*, 1717; (ed. in French, German and English by ANNA LINDE: Breitkopf & Härtel, Leipzig 1933).

Edward Dannreuther, *Musical Ornamentation:* Novello, London [n.d.].

Thurston Dart, *The Interpretation of Music:* Hutchinson, London 1954.

Arnold Dolmetsch, *The Interpretation of Music of the 17th and 18th Centuries:* Novello, London [n.d.].
(The separately printed Appendix, containing twenty-two illustrative pieces, contains invaluable examples of early keyboard fingering.)

Robert Donington, *The Interpretation of Early Music:* Faber, London 1963.

Walter Emery, *Bach's Ornaments:* Novello, London 1953.

Grove's Dictionary of Music and Musicians, 5th edition: Macmillan, London 1954.
Especially the articles by Dart on 'Notation', and by Donington on 'Baroque Interpretation', 'Dotted Notes', 'Expression', 'Fingering (keyboard)', 'Inégales', 'Ornamentation' and 'Phrasing'.

Rosamund E. M. Harding, *Origins of Musical Time and Expression*, Oxford University Press, London 1938.

Ralph Kirkpatrick, *Domenico Scarlatti:* Princeton University, Princeton 1953.

Clement Matchett's Virginal Book (1612), ed. THURSTON DART: Stainer & Bell, London 1957.
(For virginalist fingering.)

Wilfred Mellers, *François Couperin and the French Classical Tradition:* Dobson, London 1950.

Thomas Morley, *A Plain and Easy Introduction to Practical Music*, 1597; ed. R. ALEC HARMAN: Dent, London 1952.

Raymond Russell, *The Harpsichord and Clavichord:* Faber, London 1959.

Curt Sachs, *Rhythm and Tempo:* Dent, London 1953.

Domenico Scarlatti, *Sixty Sonatas*, ed. with a Preface by RALPH KIRKPATRICK: Schirmer, New York 1953.

KEYBOARD MUSIC

The Short Mesure off My Lady Wynkfylds Rownde

Source: British Museum,
MS. Royal App. 58

Anon. English
(mid-16th century)

The mid-16th century manuscript from which this piece is taken also contains the better known *Hornepype* by Hugh Aston (? 16th century), the anonymous *My Lady Careys Dompe*, and seven other shorter keyboard pieces. (Reprinted complete in *Early Keyboard Music*, vol. 1, ed. Frank Dawes: Schott, London 1951.) The three pieces named above are the earliest known genuinely idiomatic virginals music, in which the accompanying figures in the l.h. parts distinguish them clearly from the more contrapuntal organ music of the same period. The MS once belonged to Thomas Mulliner, Master of the Choristers of St. Paul's, who also owned and probably copied the important early keyboard MS now known as *The Mulliner Book*. (Reprinted in *Musica Britannica* I, ed. Denis Stevens: Stainer & Bell, London 1951.)

The *Rownde* has no barlines in the original and is written out in full. Repeat-signs are used in the present edition to save space.

In performance remember that the piece is a gay and fairly brisk dance, with a tempo of about ♩. = 60; and show clearly the unusual bar-scheme: 4 + 5 in the opening section, and 6 (2 + 2 + 2) + 4 in the contrasting section (bb. 13-22). The lack of a sustaining pedal on the virginals would automatically make the 3rd l.h. beat of each bar non-legato, and this helps to give the necessary swing to the rhythm. A possible r.h. phrasing would be the following:

[1] In the original there are no barlines; and the notes printed small in r.h. b. 7 and l.h. bb. 9 and 58 are missing.

[2] In bb. 37-38 the flat and natural to the r.h. B only appear the first time round.

Pavana: The Earle of Salisbury

Source: *Parthenia* (c. 1612/13)

WILLIAM BYRD
(1542/3-1623)

These two pieces by Byrd are taken from *Parthenia, or the Maydenhead of the first musicke that euer was printed for the Virginalls*, c. 1612/13, a collection of twenty-one pieces, of which eight are by Byrd, seven by John Bull and six by Orlando Gibbons. (Reproduced in facsimile as one of the 'Harrow Replicas', ed. O. E. Deutsch: Chiswick Press, London 1942. Reprinted complete in *Parthenia*, ed. Thurston Dart: Stainer & Bell, London 1960.)

The Pavan and Galliard were favourite dances of the period, the first slow and stately and the second a fairly quick contrast. Generally they contained three strains each, either with or without divisions; but here there are only two. They were often composed as a pair, sometimes thematically connected; and though the present Galliard is not paired with the Pavan by its title, the two pieces are neighbours in the volume and go well together in performance.

Both the 2nd-time bars of the *Pavana* are editorial. (See the Introduction, p. 15, concerning repeats.) It is possible that the last r.h. note in b. 9 should be a B crotchet, as in the bar before, instead of G natural. But the G preserves the correct shape of the phrase, with its rising fourths, and also appears in the repeat of the 2nd strain; so on the whole it seems likely that it was omitted from the original by mistake. The false-relation it makes with the G sharp at the beginning of the bar is typical of English music of this period.

The *Pavana* should be gravely expressive and predominantly legato with a tempo of ♩ = c. 80. Allow full importance to the interesting inner voices, particularly when they use direct imitation (bb. 5-7) or disguised imitation (bb. 10 & 12). It is a good plan to omit the ornamentation until the shape of the music is firmly in the player's mind and fingers; then as many or as few ornaments may be added as are compatible with the player's technique and with the touch and tone quality of his instrument.

The *Galiardo* requires more broken phrasing: ♩· ♪ ♩ ♪ ♩ ♪ ; with a tempo of ♩ = c. 80. The frequent imitative entries should be clearly defined: e.g. b. 1 bass and middle voice, b. 2 treble, and b. 3 middle voices. And notice in the second half of b. 10 and the following bar how the four-note descending figure momentarily assumes a new importance, which calls for a more cantabile tone. If all the ornaments are played they will sound sparkling on the harpsichord but rather over-crowded on the piano. It may be found advisable to omit some or even all of them; in which case the tempo might be a fraction quicker.

Reproduced by kind permission of the Huntington Library, San Marino, California.

[1] Short barlines are editorial.

Galiardo

Source: *Parthenia* (c. 1612/13)

WILLIAM BYRD

¹ In the original ♪♪♪♪♪ , which probably stood for a trill. Could be played ♪♪♪♪♪ , or with more repercussions.

C

A Gigge: Doctor Bulls My Selfe

Source: *Fitzwilliam Virginal Book*
(before 1619)

JOHN BULL
(c. 1563-1628)

The Fitzwilliam Virginal Book, from which this piece is taken, is the largest and most important extant source of virginals music. (Reprinted complete, ed. J. A. Fuller-Maitland and W. Barclay Squire: Breitkopf & Härtel, Leipzig 1899†). The manuscript, which now belongs to the Fitzwilliam Museum, Cambridge, was copied by Francis Tregian the younger during his confinement in the Fleet Prison for recusancy from 1609 until his death in 1619. It contains in all 297 pieces, by thirty-six named composers (mostly English) and others unnamed.

Bull's *Gigge*, or jig, provides examples of the Fitzwilliam Virginal Book's use of an implied but unmarked D.C., and of a redundant final breve bar. These are discussed in the Introduction, p. 15, from which it will be found that here the final bar should be omitted; and that, after the D.C., has been made, the piece should end on the 5th crotchet of the penultimate bar.

The tempo is a brisk two-in-a-bar of ♩. = c. 72. At this speed all the ornaments are quite practical on the piano. The phrasing suggested by the virginal's lack of pedals would be as follows: ; with the occasional displaced accents underline thus:

† Low-priced reprint published by Dover Books, New York 1968.

¹ Short barlines are editorial.

Reproduced by kind permission of the Fitzwilliam Museum, Cambridge.

² Original MS:- ³ See Introduction, p. 15

Tell mee Daphne

Source: *Fitzwilliam Virginal Book*
(before 1619)

GILES FARNABY
(c. 1565-1640)

For details of the Fitzwilliam Virginal Book, from which this piece is taken, see the Note on Bull's *Gigge*. Farnaby's *Tell mee Daphne* is a typical example, in all but its conciseness, of one of the favourite forms of the virginalists: a set of variations on a popular tune or folk-song. As the tunes were well known to contemporary listeners there was no need for them to appear in a simple, unornamented form before the variations began; thus the pieces always plunge directly into what we would now call Variation 1.

The ending shows the redundant final breve bar so often found in the Fitzwilliam Virginal Book. This peculiarity is discussed on p. 15 of the Introduction, from which it will be found that the final bar should here be omitted.

The words of *Tell mee Daphne* are no longer known. (The first half of the tune of *Go no more a-rushing* is almost identical with it, and both words and music of this are reprinted in B. H. Bronson's *The Traditional Tunes of the Child Ballads*, vol. 1: Princeton 1959.) Farnaby's setting suggests a mood of gentle melancholy. The simplicity of the opening should not beguile one into playing the piece too quickly. Look ahead to bb. 9-10 in Variation 2, and set your tempo by the possibility of negotiating the awkward r.h. jumps neatly and cleanly. These, and the remaining semiquaver passages, become easier and more musical when it is realised that the majority of them must be phrased from the second semiquaver of the four-note groups: e.g. in l.h. b. 12 there are two phrases, and in b. 13 there are four, and each begins on the second semiquaver of a group, not the first. The tempo should be about ♩ = 76; and there needs to be a slight easing up at the end of each Variation. The surprising accidentals in r.h. b. 15 are not misprints: they appear thus in the MS.

Reproduced by kind permission of the Fitzwilliam Museum, Cambridge.

[omit]²

[Fine]

¹ Somesuch spread chord as:    ² See Introduction, p. 15

Fantazia of Foure Parts

Source: *Parthenia* (c. 1612/13)

ORLANDO GIBBONS
(1583-1625)

This magnificent work is one of the finest of the virginalist Fantasies or Fancies. In breadth of conception it far surpasses any other of the pieces in *Parthenia*, from which it is taken. (See the Note on Byrd's *Pavana* for details of this important collection of virginals music.)

The instrumental Fantasy or Fancy was modelled on the 16th century unaccompanied vocal Motet, in which successive portions of a text were treated in imitative counterpoint, each section having a new musical subject known as a 'point of imitation', or simply a 'point'. The end of one section generally overlapped the beginning of the next; but sometimes the sections were self-contained.

In Gibbons' *Fantazia* there are in all six points, the beginning of each of which is shown in the present edition by the editorial marks P. 1, P. 2, etc. The sections overlap throughout, except at the end of P. 3 where the music pauses on a dotted minim before launching into P. 4. This pause is important architecturally, for it divides the spacious opening two-thirds of the work from the more urgent concluding third.

In performance the player should aim at the expressive and plastic dynamics natural to a group of singers or a clavichord, rather than the 'terraced' dynamics of the harpsichord; and he should strive throughout to preserve the individuality of the contrapuntal parts and their continually changing dynamic relationship. Bearing in mind the same vocal analogy, he will find that the rise and fall of dynamics is conditioned by the melodic and harmonic shape of each phrase and section, and of the work as a whole.

If we analyse P. 1, for example, it will be found to fall into three parts each closed by a perfect cadence: on A in b. 17, on E in b. 25, and again on A in b. 34. The opening is grave and quiet, with a tempo of ♩ = c. 52. As the voices enter successively there is a gradual increase in the harmonic interest, which is then relaxed in the cadence of b. 16-17. The second part quickly becomes less dark in colour through its shift of tessitura and the high treble entry of the subject in b. 18; and this is rounded off by a longer but less complete relaxation to the cadence b. 24-25. The third part echoes the second at a still higher level and provides the climax of the whole of P. 1 with the treble entry in b. 26. This in its turn relaxes to the final cadence of the section, in bb. 33-34, where we are now ready for the entry of P. 2 in the second half of b. 34.

A similar analysis of the remaining sections of the work will provide the player with the bare bones of his interpretation. He must then proceed to articulate these by discovering the relationship of one section to another.

Thus P. 2 will be found to start on a higher dynamic level than P. 1, and to fall back to where it began. P. 3 begins where P. 2 leaves off, and reaches in b. 87 both the main climax of the opening of the work and the secondary climax of the work as a whole. This falls away somewhat to b. 96, but rather quickly builds up again, by means of closer rythmic detail, to the beginning of b. 104. The cadence bars 104-5 and the dotted minim chord mentioned earlier relax the tension and round off the first large unit consisting of P. 1, P. 2 & P. 3. (It will be found that the structural importance of the pause requires a slight and gradual broadening of the tempo, beginning at b. 103.)

The concluding third of the work, with its greater rhythmic urgency, calls for a very slight increase in tempo, say ♩ = c. 60. A drop in dynamics at the beginning of P. 4 is also required, to allow for the long build-up which carries through (with local fluctuations) to the triumphant tenor entry of P. 6 in b. 142. (Note how rhythmic variety is achieved by the cross-accentuation of P. 5: ♪ ♫ ♩ ♩ ♩ |, which provides such a vigorous contrast to the cantabile phrasing of the earlier points: and note how the main flow of rhythm is re-established by the three solid minim chords of bb. 132-3, echoed a fifth higher in bb. 139-40.) A gradual broadening of the tempo from b. 153 will not only underline the last group of entries of P. 6, but will at the same time help to bring this rich and splendid *Fantazia* to a fittingly solemn close.

[1] Short barlines are editorial.
[2] P.1, P. 2 etc. are editorial, and show where the various "points" or subjects initiate new sections of the work.
[3] Demisemiquavers in original, perhaps indicating trills?

P. 3

[3] Demisemiquavers in original, perhaps indicating trills?

D

[4] Barline in original (at the end of a line).

Style and Interpretation (Vol. I)   34

Gavott

Source: *A choice Collection of Lessons for the Harpsichord, Spinnet, etc.* (1704)

JOHN BLOW
(1648/9-1708)

This *Gavott* is taken from a collection of Blow's harpsichord pieces published four years before his death. (Complete reprint in: John Blow, *Six Suites*, ed. Howard Ferguson; Stainer & Bell, London 1965.) It also appeared five years earlier in a slightly simpler, untitled version in *The Second Part of Musick's Handmaid*, 1689, a collection of pieces by Blow, Purcell and others published by Henry Playford. (Reprinted complete, ed. Thurston Dart: Stainer & Bell, London 1958.)

It is interesting to find that the haphazard notation of repeats used by the virginalists was carried over into this later period. (The repeat-signs in the present edition are editorial, as is the 1st-time bar.) There is also the same ambiguity about details of repeats. Should the final repeat be made as shown by the editorial marks? Or should it go back to the up-beat in b. 5, with the equivalent up-beat in b. 13 left out the first time round? The editor has chosen the first solution, but others may prefer the second.

In performance remember that the Gavotte was a less staid dance at this period than later. A speed of ♩ = c. 80 should be about right. The pairs of quavers should be light and dancing throughout, with phrasing something after the following pattern:

In l.h. b. 9 do not attempt a legato between the two halves of the bar. The fact that it is written like this means that a break between the F-sharp and G is intended.

¹ 1st time bar and all repeat signs are editorial.

Reproduced by kind permission of the Director of the Royal College of Music, London.

Style and Interpretation (Vol. I)

35

Prelude *(Suite No. 2)*

Source: *A Choice Collection of Lessons*
for the Harpsichord or Spinnet (1696)

HENRY PURCELL
(1658/9-1695)

Purcell's *A Choice Collection of Lessons*, which was issued by his widow Frances a year
after his death, contains eight Suites and a few separate pieces. (Complete harpsichord
works in: Henry Purcell, *Eight Suites* and *Miscellaneous Keyboard Pieces*, ed. Howard
Ferguson; Stainer & Bell, London 1968 (2nd ed.).) The Suites are made up of three or
four movements in a single key; generally a Prelude, Almand, Corant and Saraband or
Minuet. (Purcell's Saraband is a fairly brisk movement, so it provides a perfectly satisfactory ending to a Suite.)

The opening movement of the 2nd Suite is perhaps the most beautiful of all the Preludes.
It is a smoothly flowing piece of about ♩ = 80, in which a predominantly legato touch is
suggested by the r.h. notation in the second half of b. 4. No very wide dynamic variation is
required; but the rise and fall should follow the melodic and harmonic shape of the phrases.
The first long phrase must be carried right to the beginning of b. 11, before which a fraction
of time is needed to allow for the overlap with the following phrase. Note, too, the continually
changing length of the shorter phrases within the longer units: e.g. the unexpected groupings
in bb. 6-7 of $\frac{2}{4}$, $\frac{3}{4}$ and $\frac{3}{4}$; and the shift in b. 14 from half-bar phrases to a cadence-phrase
lasting a bar and a half.

[1] The penultimate semiquaver in the l.h. is F in the original, not G; but this is probably a misprint.

[2] B. 17, r.h., note 12: D, not E.   [3] B. 18, r.h., note 3: B (flat), not A.   [4] B. 18, l.h., note 8: C, not B (flat).

A New Ground

Source: *The Second Part of Musick's Handmaid* (1689)

HENRY PURCELL

This *Ground* is taken from *The Second Part of Musick's Handmaid*. (See the Note on Blow's *Gavott*.) Like many other pieces in the volume, it has no composer's name attached; but it is undoubtedly by Purcell, for it is a keyboard version of his song *Here the Deities Attend*, from the ode *Welcome to all the Pleasures*. In the preface to *Musick's Handmaid* the publisher, Henry Playford, states that the pieces have been 'carefully Revised and Corrected by the said Mr. Henry Purcell'.

Typical of Purcell is the way in which the phrases of the r.h. 'solo', beginning on the 4th beat of b. 3, generally overlap the three-bar phrases of the ground-bass: a device which ensures rhythmic and harmonic variety. On a two-manual harpsichord this solo would be played on one manual, while the l.h. ground-bass and the r.h. syncopated figure that sometimes goes with it would be played on the other. This contrast should be carefully preserved on the piano. Thus the opening two-and-a-half bars should suggest a discreet yet sensitively modulated accompaniment, while the r.h. cantabile should be played with all the authority and expressive power natural to a soloist. (Note that the last r.h. note of b. 7 and the first of b. 8 are accompaniment, not solo.) The lay-out of the l.h. part in bb. 4-6, etc., suggests that the ground-bass should be played *legatissimo* throughout. The speed should be a leisurely eight-in-a-bar, say about ♪ = 80.

[1]*Musick's Handmaid* gives C for the second quaver. The more probable B comes from *Here the Deities Attend.*

Gigue *(Sonata No. 6)*

Source: *VIII Sonatas or Lessons for the Harpsichord* (1756)

THOMAS AUGUSTINE ARNE
(1710-1778)

Arne published eight Sonatas for harpsichord. (Reprinted in facsimile, ed. G. Beechey & T. Dart; Stainer & Bell. London 1969.) The last of them is a rather dull set of variations on a minuet by some unnamed composer, but rest are delightful little works of two, three or four movements each. The present *Gigue* is the finale of a two-movement Sonata whose opening movement is a ¾ *Affettuoso* in G minor.

In performance it should be remembered that the mid-18th century *Presto* was slower than the *Presto* of today or even of Mozart's time. ♩. = 112-120 should be quite quick enough. In bb. 16-19 the two legato phrases begin on the fourth quaver of bb. 16 & 18; while the similar passage in the second half (bb. 53-56) provides amusing variety by splitting the first phrase into two. Do not feel that the many duplicated phrases must be treated as echo-effects: this would merely break up the line unnecessarily and make the music sound short-winded. The small notes in the l.h. of bb. 39-42 are editorial, and show the sort of filling-in that was left to the performer at this period. The use or omission of such additions depends not only on the texture of the music, but also on the tone of the instrument used and the resonance of the room in which it is played. A possible phrasing-pattern would be:

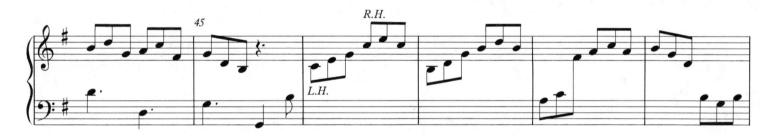

Sarabande

Source: *Les Pièces de Clauessin* (1670)

JACQUES CHAMPION de CHAMBONNIÈRES
(c. 1602–c. 1672)

This *Sarabande* is taken from the first of two small volumes of harpsichord pieces published two years before the composer's death. (Reprint ed. Thurston Dart: Oiseau-Lyre, Monaco 1970.)

As in Purcell, the speed should be rather quicker than that of a Bach Sarabande: say about ♩ = 80. The quavers in l.h. bb. 2-3, r.h. bb. 11 & 13, and similar places, should be treated as *notes inégales* (see Introduction, p. 18). The rhythms suggested above or below the stave at their first appearance are only rough approximations; for the player's discretion, or *bon goût*, must always be the arbiter where these subtle rhythmic alterations are concerned.

It would be in keeping with the style of the period to play the r.h. cadential chords in bb. 12, 16 & 24 as arpeggios, either upwards or downwards, even though they are not so marked.

The cross above the r.h. F in b. 19 here stands for a *port de voix*. In Chambonnières' list of ornaments this is explained as ♪♪ ; but it seems likely that the explanation given is a misprint for ♪ , which is the usual form of the ornament, and that used by Chambonnières' own pupil d'Anglebert.

[1]The shake is engraved between the 2nd beat D and E in the original. B. 15 suggests that it belongs to the D.

Gavotte

Source: *Pièces de Clavecin* (1689)

JEAN HENRI D'ANGLEBERT
(1635-1691)

In the Gavotte of this period the beat was normally something between 98 and 152 to either the crotchet or the minim. Here, however, the harmonic movement and closeness of rhythmic detail require it to be about ♪= 132. (*cf.* the Introduction, p. 9, under *Tempo.*) This suggests that the indication *lentement* has been omitted from the original edition by mistake; particularly as it is attached to d'Anglebert's remaining Gavottes in the same volume. (Complete reprint ed. M. Roesgen-Champion: Société Française de Musicologie, Paris 1934.)

Because of the slow tempo one should treat the semiquavers as *notes inégales*, instead of the quavers as normally expected in 2-time (see Introduction, p. 18).

A *Petite Reprise* is often found in French music of this period (see b. 17). It is a short coda in which the last few bars of the piece are played for a third time, following the normal repeat of the second half, which was called the *Reprise*.

Reprise

[Petite reprise]¹

¹ See Note above.

La Convalescente

(26me Ordre)

Source: *4me Livre de Pièces*
de Clavecin (1730)

FRANÇOIS COUPERIN
(1668-1733)

This splendid piece is the opening movement of the last but one of Couperin's Ordres or Suites. (Complete reprint ed. Kenneth Gilbert: Heugel, Paris 1969-71; also ed. Maurice Cauchie, revised Thurston Dart: Oiseau-Lyre, Monaco 1970)

Note that Couperin's grouping of notes often implies phrasing: e.g. in r.h. bb. 16-17 the three isolated semiquavers on the 1st and 3rd beats mark the ends of phrases, and should be separated from the following three-note groups. Their fulness also implies an accent, which is best achieved on the piano by a very quick arpeggio. The tempo should be about ♩ = 60.

The low C(sharp) and F(sharp) at the end of, respectively, the 1st and the 2nd half are not in the original, though they seem to be required musically. Their absence is *not* due to the limitations of a short-octave keyboard, as suggested in the 1st edition of this anthology, for the C-sharp is used in another movement of the same suite, and the compass of many French harpsichords extended downwards chromatically to F-natural an octave below the bass stave. The two stems to the first l.h. crotchet in b. 11 do suggest, however, that there was originally a downward-stemmed note on the 2nd beat, and that this and the low F-sharp in the final bar were probably left out by an oversight of the engraver.

[1]The ties are thus in the original; but logically they should start at the grace-note.

Les Ondes *(Rondeau)*

(5me Ordre)

Source: *Pièces de Clavecin*
[1er livre] (1713)

FRANÇOIS COUPERIN

Les Ondes is the final piece in the last Ordre of Couperin's First Book of harpsichord pieces. (For complete reprints, see the Note on *La Convalescente*.) In the original the repetitions of the main theme are not written out in full, but merely indicated by D.C. signs as was then customary with rondos. (This old type of lay-out is reproduced in the present edition of Rameau's *La Triomphante*, p. 52.)

The indication *sans lenteur* must only be taken as a warning against dragging. The tempo cannot possibly be fast, if only because of the number of ornaments that have to be fitted in; and these, unlike the more haphazard ornamentation of the English virginalists, are a carefully calculated part of the music. *The Waves* of the title will be convincingly suggested by a gently undulating two-in-a-bar of ♩. = c. 58-60.

The ornament ⤳ when preceded by a slur ⤳ is properly realised thus: ⤳ . But sometimes it will be found that there is not sufficient time for the tie, so that it becomes necessary to simplify the rhythm to ⤳ . (This interpretation is, indeed, given by Dandrieu, as can be seen from the table of ornaments on p. 17 of the Introduction.) Here it may be found best to begin with the simplified version; then, after some practice, the player can change over to the more accurate form of the ornament, with its fascinating effect of a subtle rubato.

The fingering given here is Couperin's and is taken from his *L'Art de Toucher le Clavecin*, 1717 (see Introduction, p. 11). Though the player of today may not wish to follow this exactly, it provides nevertheless a revealing insight into the phrasing required. For example, in b. 66 Couperin clearly wants this: ⤳ . (Note that the finger given to an ornament applies to its *main* note.) And in b. 72 he wants the descending scale phrased thus: ⤳ .

The wedge-shaped dash in the 3rd Couplet (b. 44 onwards) means an *aspiration*, or shortened note. Again this is underlined by the frequent use of the same finger for the following note.

In the 4th Couplet the semiquavers should be treated as *notes inégales* (see Introduction, p. 18). But do not play all the pairs identically, as this would be monotonous. Show the phrase construction by leaning rather more on the beginnings of phrases: e.g. on the second quaver beat in bb. 60-62, and the first and fourth beats in bb. 63-65, so that the contrast between full-bar and half-bar phrases is made apparent.

Gracieusement, sans lenteur

¹ See Note above concerning this ornament.

E

2e couplet

3e couplet

4e couplet

La Triomphante

Source: *Nouvelles Suites de Pièces*
de Clavecin (c. 1728)

JEAN PHILIPPE RAMEAU
(1683-1764)

Rameau published in all four sets of solo harpsichord pieces (complete reprint ed. Erwin R. Jacobi: Bärenreiter, Kassel 1958). *La Triomphante* is taken from the third volume, which was published about 1728. Like all rondos of the period, it was printed with D.C. signs instead of full written-out repeats of the main theme, a layout which is here reproduced exactly. The repeat of the main theme is only made the first time round. This is followed by the *1ᵉ Reprise* (Couperin would have called it the *1ᵉʳ Couplet*) plus a repeat of the main theme; which is then followed by the *2ᵉ Reprise* and a final repeat of the main theme. The exact details of the ending are left to the player's taste and judgement. He could finish in b. 12, with the four final quavers held on a pause; or he could hold on the r.h. A for an extra bar, and finish the l.h. on the low A of b. 13.

The wayward charm of *notes inégales* would be out of place in such a vigorous and forthright piece (see Introduction, p. 18); the quavers should therefore be played evenly throughout.

The tempo is an *Allegro* of about ♩ = 84.

Reproduced by kind permission of the British Museum

[2e Reprise]

D.C. al Fine

D.C. al Fine

L'Enharmonique

Source: *Nouvelles Suites de Pièces de Clavecin* (c. 1728)

JEAN PHILIPPE RAMEAU

This astonishing piece also comes from the third of Rameau's four sets of harpsichord solos. (*cf.* Note on *La Triomphante*.) In the context of early 18th century French keyboard music its harmonies are startling, as Rameau himself remarked, but they are also convincing, beautiful and highly expressive.

The use of *notes inégales* is particularly interesting. In 2-time the quavers would normally be played unequally; but here it is the semiquavers, as can be seen from the contrary indication in bb. 10, 20 & 68: *hardiment, sans altérer la mesure (boldly, without altering the rhythm)*. The word *gracieusement* indicates a return to unequal semiquavers.

The wedge-shaped dash above the 3rd demi-semiquaver in bb. 10 & 20 indicates an *aspiration* or shortened note (*cf.* Couperin's *Les Ondes*, p. 49). There may not appear to be much time for this at ♪ = 100, which is roughly the speed of the piece. But experiment will show that a break is perfectly possible if the first three notes are phrased together, and the last of the three is used as a sort of springboard to project the hand on to the fourth note. The result, as with *notes inégales*, is a subtle rubato which it would be difficult to notate more clearly.

In the original edition the rhythm of bb. 31-32 and all similar passages is shown consistently as [r.h. / l.h. musical example].

This may or may not mean that Rameau regarded the two demi-semiquavers at the beginning of each bar as grace-notes. The notation given in the present edition has been preferred, since it is similar in effect and is at the same time more precise.

Gracieusement

hardiment, sans altérer la mesure [1]

[1] See Note above.

gracieusement

hardiment

gracieusement

Reprise

45

50

55

3

60

65

hardiment

70

gracieusement

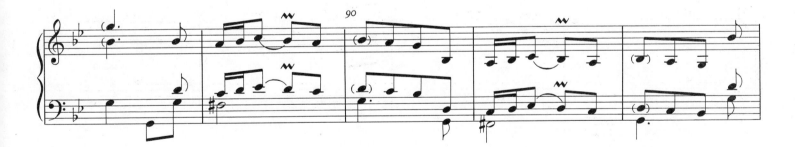

La Lyre d'Orphée

Source: *2me Livre de Pièces de Clavecin* (1728)

JEAN FRANÇOIS DANDRIEU
(1684-1740)

Dandrieu published three volumes of harpsichord pieces during his lifetime (no complete modern reprint exists), from the second of which this piece is taken.

It provides an example of yet another kind of *note inégale*, for the word *piqué* (sometimes *pointé*) shows that here the dotted-crotchet-and-quaver rhythms should be double-dotted. But it is important to remember that this does not apply to syncopations. Hence the top part in r.h. bb. 18 & 21 should be played as written and *not* double-dotted.

The lingering beauty of the suspensions in the *Reprise*, coupled with the indication *Grave*, suggest a tempo of about ♩ = 60.

Reprise

Petite Reprise[1]

[1] See Note to d'Anglebert *Gavotte*, p. 44.

L'Hirondelle

Source: 1er *Livre de Pièces de Clavecin* (1735)

LOUIS CLAUDE DAQUIN
(1694-1772)

Daquin published only one volume entirely devoted to harpsichord pieces. (No complete modern reprint exists.) A second volume entitled *Nouveau Livre de Noëls*, also published in 1735, was described as being for organ and harpsichord; but as five of the twelve pieces have pedal parts, these at least must have been intended primarily for organ. *L'Hirondelle* comes from the first of the two volumes.

It is uncertain whether *notes inégales* are intended here. Semiquavers are normally treated as *inégales* in $\frac{2}{4}$ time; but one of the exceptions to the rule is when a piece is in a very quick tempo. If *L'Hirondelle* is to sound like darting swallows, as is obviously intended, it must be played at about ♩ = 100; and this leaves little time for the pairing of semiquavers. A more musical alternative would be to lean slightly on the first semiquaver of each sub-phrase, thus providing rhythmic variety and underlining the contrasting phrase-lengths. For example, the first four bars of the r.h. part might be stressed thus:

with the l.h. part treated similarly.

In the original no D.C. of the first part is marked; but one was always understood in pieces consisting of a distinct 1st and 2nd part. If a repeat of the whole 1st part seems too long in performance, a satisfactory ending can be made in b. 38.

It will be found best to finger the cadential ornaments after this pattern: with the change to the 5th finger on the last semiquaver of the bar. It would be in the style of the period to shorten this note, as shown.

2e couplet

[Fine]

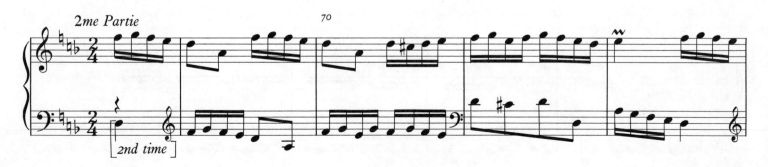

Reprise

[*D.C. al Fine*]

¹ Thus in the original; but  is more probable.